Name :

....

WHY THIS COLORING BOOK IS VERY IMPORTANT TO YOUR KIDS?

Your child goes off to preschool, a master of scribbling. Then she hands you a piece of artwork that shows she's tried to color inside the lines for the first time. It's a big moment — and you deserve to do your proud parent dance as you tape that page to the fridge .

That switch in coloring skills is a milestone for children because" ,it shows that their motor skills and cognitive skills are developing says Rachel Annunziato, Ph.D., an associate professor of " psychology at Fordham University in New York .

WHY THIS HANDWRITING BOOK IS VERY IMPORTANT TO YOUR KIDS?

Handwriting is an important part of literacy and an essential skill for life

For toddlers and preschoolers, handwriting is about drawing and scribbling with crayons and chalk. Older children learn formal handwriting at school

Everyday activities like drawing, writing shopping lists and writing on cards can help your child learn to write

Learn & Coloring

Part 1

A

B

C

D

E

F

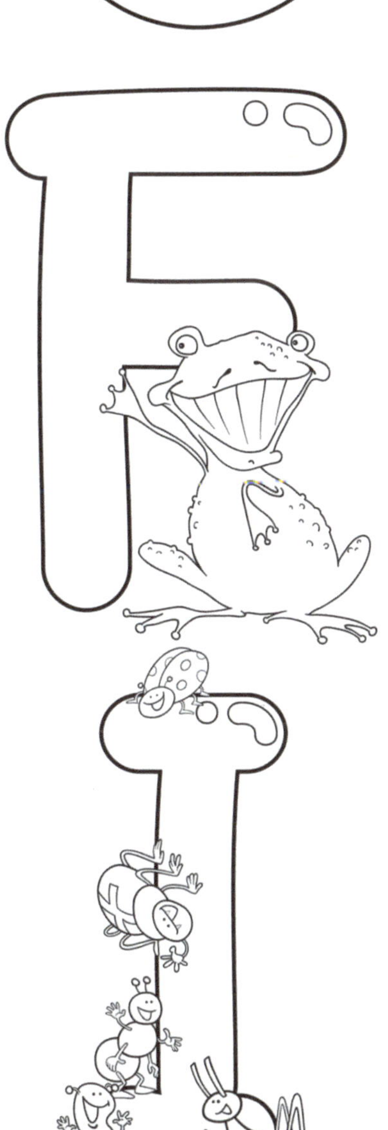

G

H

I

LEARN & FUN

ABC game for kids

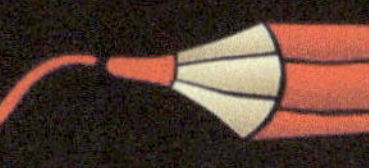

LEARN & FUN

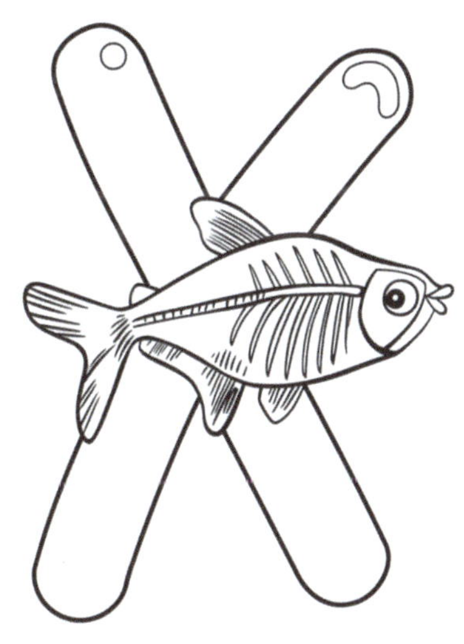

Learn & Coloring

Part 2

ABC game for kids

alligator

Bb
ABC game
for kids

Bear

Cc

ABC game for kids

cat

Dd

ABC game
for kids

dog

E e

ABC game for kids

elephant

Ff

ABC game for kids

flamingo

G g

ABC game for kids

giraffe

H h
ABC game
for kids

hippo

ABC game for kids

iguana

J j

ABC game
for kids

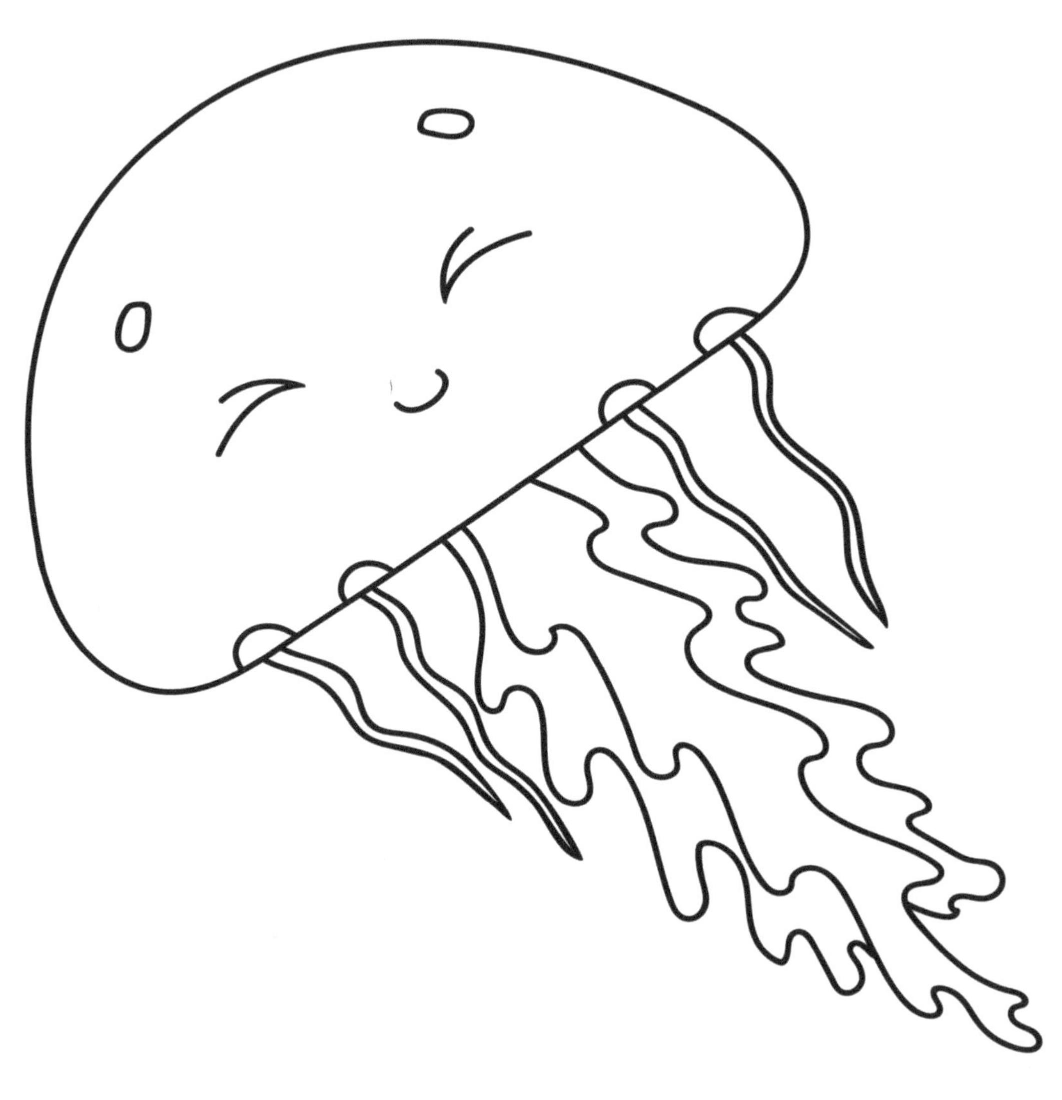

jellyFish

K k

ABC game for kids

kangaroo

Ll

ABC game
for kids

lion

ABC game for kids

monkey

N n

narwhal

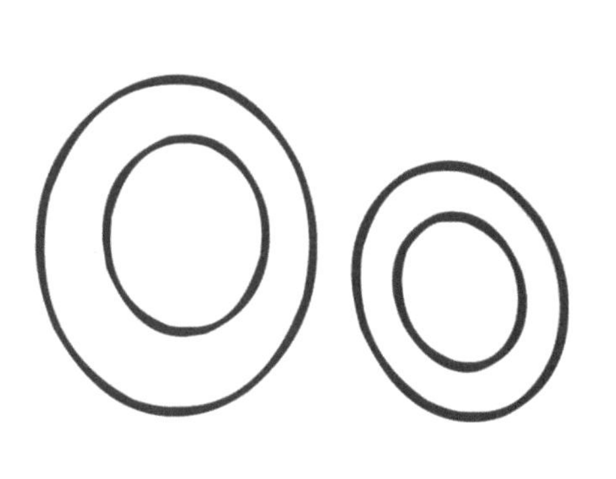

ABC game for kids

owl

P p

ABC game for kids

penguin

ABC game for kids

quail

Rr

ABC game
for kids

rhino

ABC game for kids

sloth

Tt

ABC game
for kids

tiger

Uu

ABC game
for kids

unicorn

V v

ABC game
for kids

vulture

Ww

ABC game
for kids

wolf

Xx

Xerus

Y y

ABC game
for kids

yak

Zz

zebra

Learn & Coloring

123
Game for kids

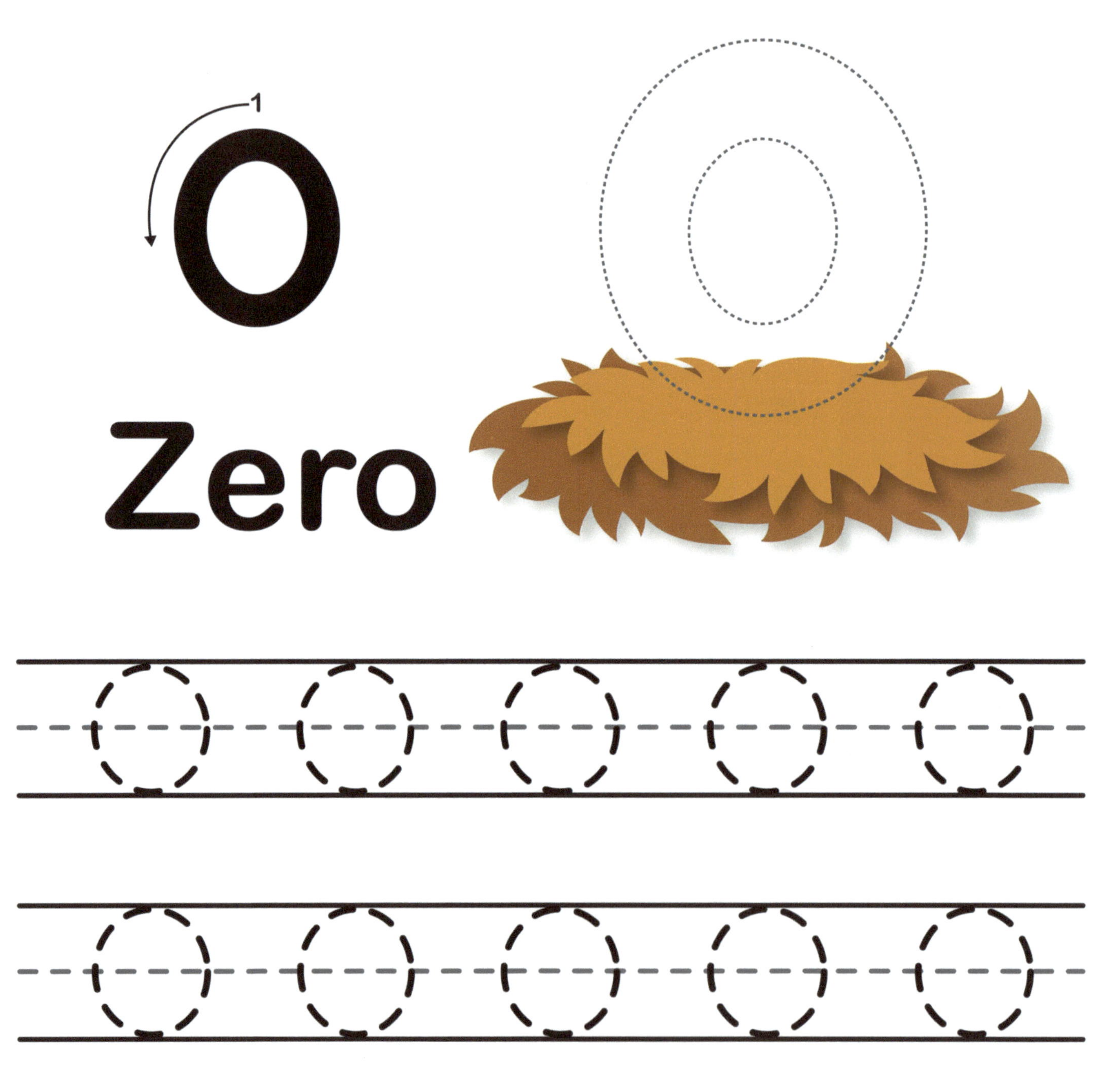

123
Game for kids

123
Game for kids

Two

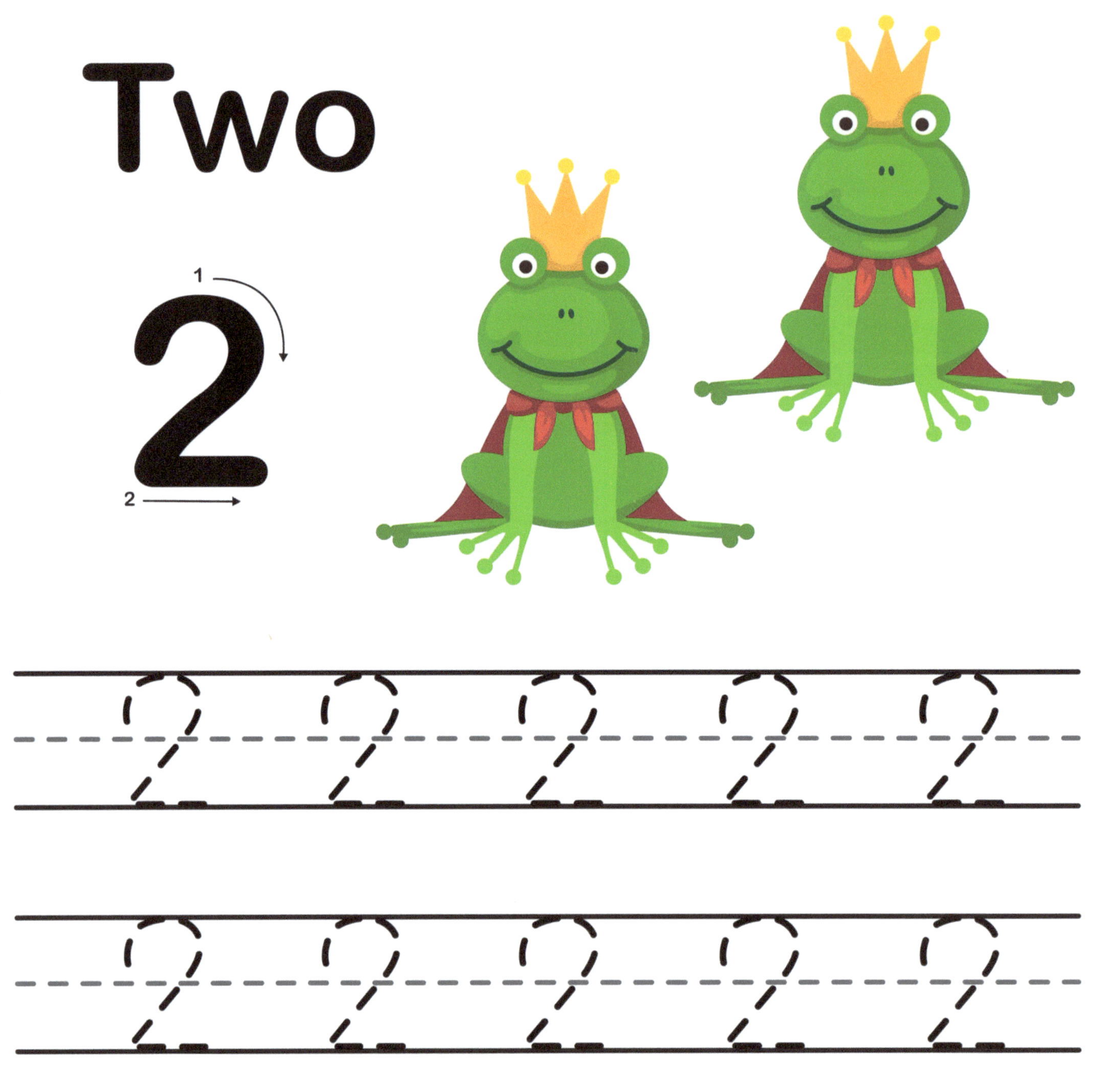

123
Game for kids

Three

3

123
Game for kids

123
Game for kids

123
Game for kids

6

Six

123
Game for kids

123
Game for kids

Eight

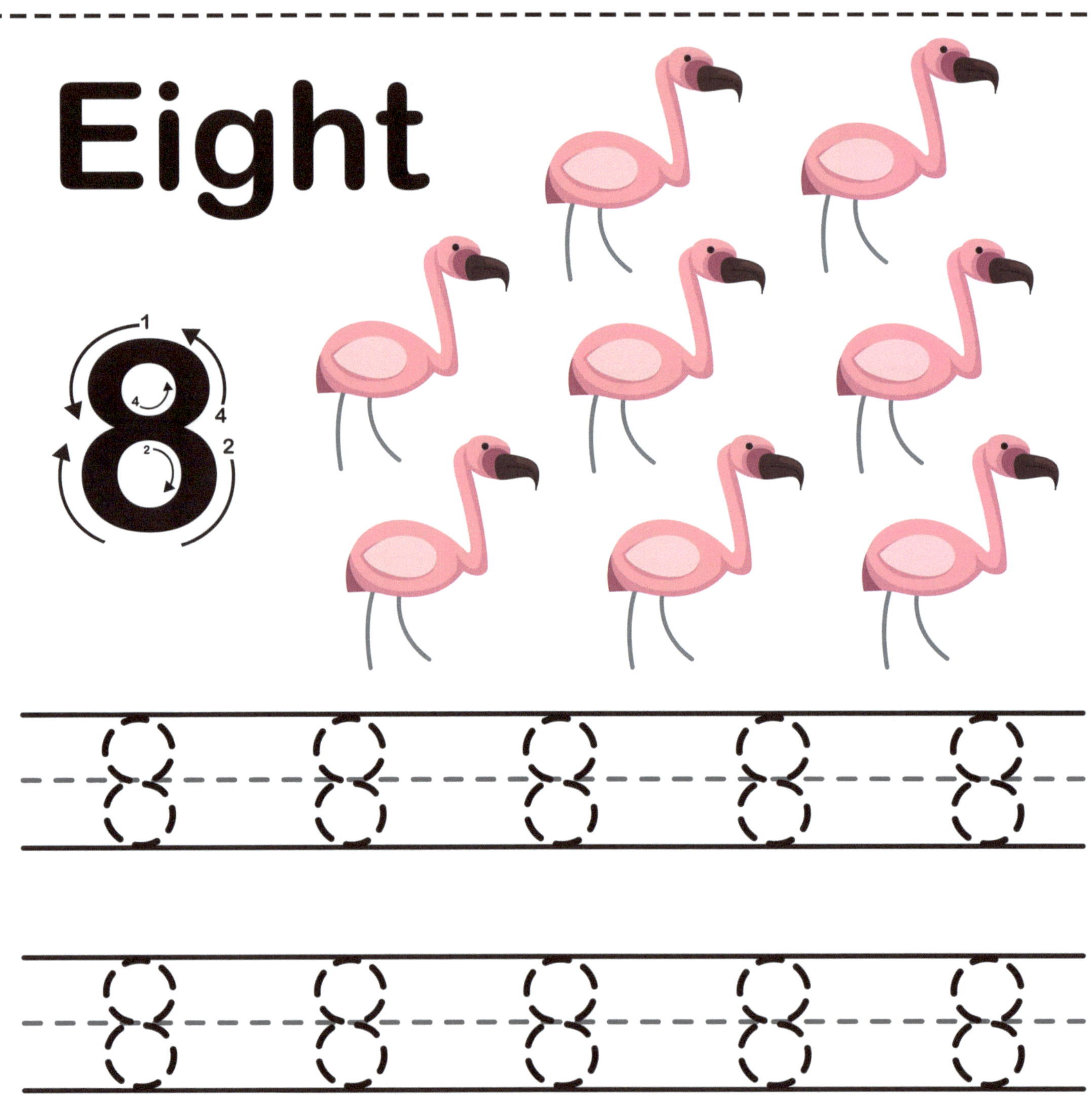

123
Game for kids

1
Art Award
Name : ....
Signature :
Date : ...... / ...... / ....

www.ingramcontent.com/pod-product-compliance
Lightning Source LLC
Chambersburg PA
CBHW040145240726
48664CB00002B/601